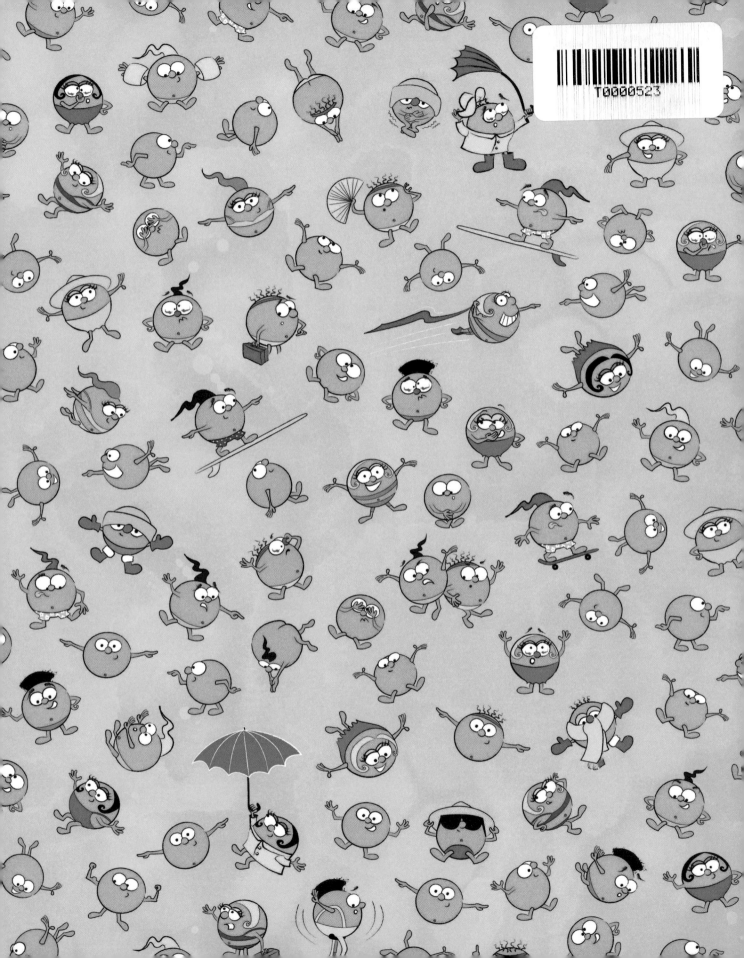

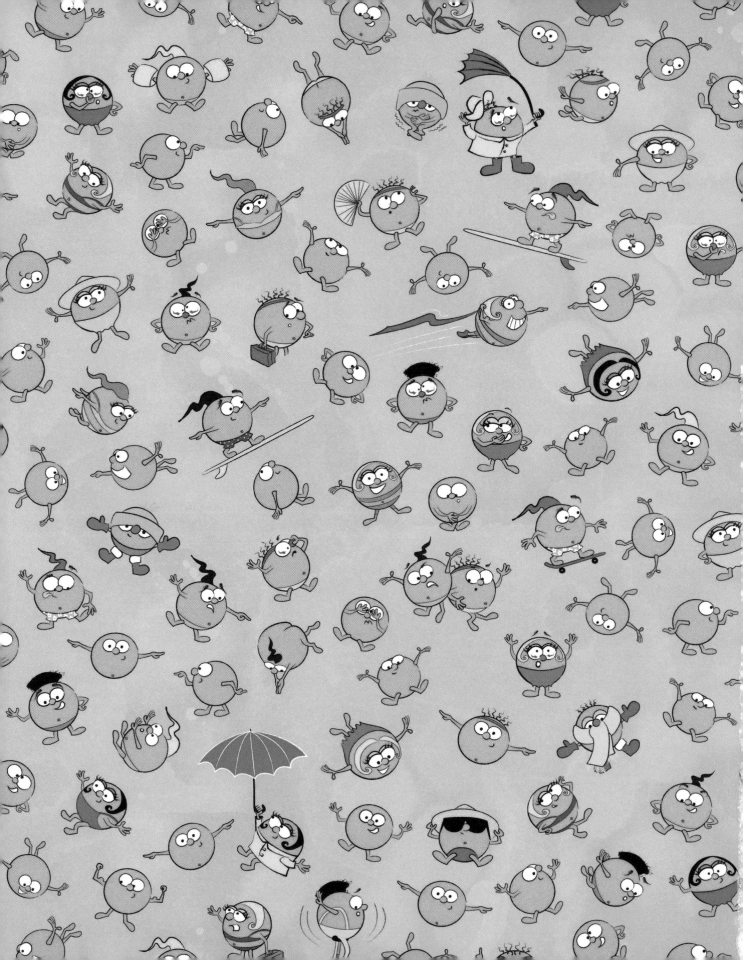

The Everywhere Atom

A Journey through the Carbon Cycle and Climate Change

by Christine Shearer

Illustrated by Kaz Clarke

Published in 2024 by
Haymarket Books
P.O. Box 180165
Chicago, IL 60618
773-583-7884
www.haymarketbooks.org
info@haymarketbooks.org

ISBN: 978-1-64259-969-5

Distributed to the trade in the US through Consortium Book Sales and Distribution (www.cbsd.com) and internationally through Ingram Publisher Services International (www.ingramcontent.com).

This book was published with the generous support of Lannan Foundation, Wallace Action Fund, and Marguerite Casey Foundation.

Special discounts are available for bulk purchases by organizations and institutions. Please email info@haymarketbooks.org for more information.

Cover artwork, cover design, interior artwork, and interior design by Kaz Clarke.

Library of Congress Cataloging-in-Publication data is available.

10 9 8 7 6 5 4 3 2 1

Christine Shearer, PhD, is a research manager at the Climate Imperative Foundation, where she analyzes initiatives and identifies policies that most effectively meet energy and climate goals. Her peer-reviewed research has appeared in publications such as *AGU Advances* and *Earth's Future*, and she is author of *Kivalina: A Climate Change Story*.

Kaz Clarke is an artist, illustrator, and graphic designer based in Australia whose previous work includes *The Whimsical Wisdom of Phoebe*. She has also illustrated other children's books, such as *Skadoodle & Snug's Magnificent Plan*.

Printed in Canada

This is carbon. It is an atom, the most basic building block that makes up everything around you. Atoms are too small to see without a special microscope, but you can find carbon atoms in all sorts of things, like plants, animals, rocks, and invisible gases in the air.

The carbon atom may be small,
but it's actually very strong.

Carbon atoms are tiny but everywhere.
And together they have a superpower:
they can make the whole Earth hot or cold!

Get your elbow
out of my butt!

How?

Surrounding Earth is a thin blanket of gases known as the atmosphere. In the atmosphere carbon atoms join with oxygen atoms to make the gas carbon dioxide. Together, these atoms absorb heat from the sun and warm the planet.

When there is a lot of
carbon in the atmosphere,
Earth gets hot.

You're so hot!

I know...

When there is less carbon in the atmosphere, Earth cools down.

I can't feel my butt.

The temperature of the planet shapes the weather. The weather over long periods of time is known as the climate.

Hundreds of millions of years ago when the dinosaurs lived, there was a lot of carbon in the atmosphere. The carbon made Earth so hot the planet had no ice! The weather was hot all year long, even during winter.

Hundreds of thousands of years ago when the wooly mammoths lived, there was much less carbon in the atmosphere. Earth's climate was cold. Ice grew and grew at the tips of the planet, the North and South Poles, which get less sunlight. The growth of ice sheets at both poles is known as an ice age.

How did Earth's climate change so much, from hot during the time of dinosaurs to an ice age full of wooly mammoths?

I'm everywhere!

The answer is carbon. Carbon does not stay as one thing forever. It changes shape, from a gas to rock to plants to all sorts of things. Carbon's journey is called the carbon cycle.

When the dinosaurs lived, Earth had a lot of volcanic activity. The volcanoes erupted tons of melted rock and carbon dioxide from deep below Earth's surface. With all the volcanic activity, there was a lot of carbon in the atmosphere. It made Earth hot!

12

But not all carbon stays in the atmosphere. In the air some carbon combines with rainwater, making the water acidic. As the rainwater falls, the acid slowly breaks down the land into tiny rocks and minerals. The minerals and carbon flow down rivers into the ocean.

Carbon is so hard to catch!

In the ocean, sea creatures turn the minerals and carbon into hard, protective shells for them to live inside. This is called calcium carbonate.

When the sea creatures die, they sink to the seafloor, taking their carbon shells with them. As more sea creatures die and sink, the bottom layers get smashed under the top layers and slowly turn into rock.

Carbon that was once in the air and warming the planet is now rock on the seafloor, where it does not warm the planet.

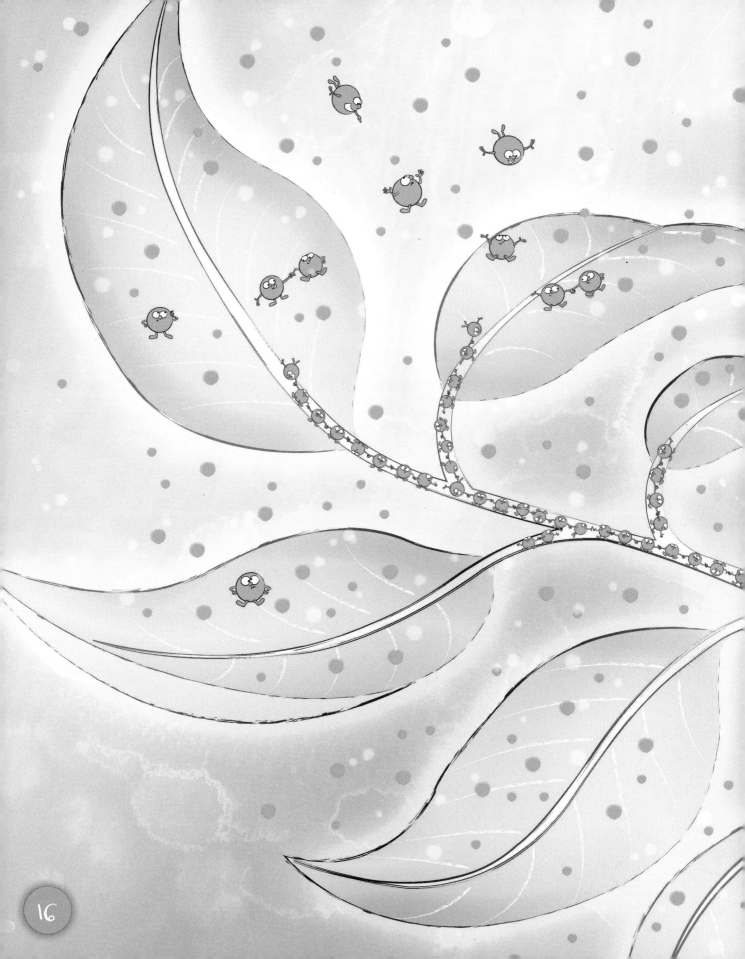

Some carbon is also taken out of the atmosphere by plants. Plants use their leaves like little solar panels to absorb sunlight energy. The energy is used to build chains of carbon and other atoms to make up the plant's leaves and stems. This process is called photosynthesis.

After photosynthesis, the carbon becomes part of the plant, filled with solar energy from the sun.

Animals cannot make their own food through photosynthesis, so they eat plants for energy. Animals breathe the carbon back out into the atmosphere, where plants can use it again. Or sometimes the carbon comes out in other ways!

Ugh, what's that smell?

Fart!

Burp!

But sometimes plants are buried before they are eaten.
If the temperature and conditions are just right, buried
plants are squeezed underground into fossil fuels.

Fossil fuels contain the carbon-rich energy of prehistoric life.
They take millions of years to form. Coal (a rock), oil (a liquid),
and methane (a gas) are all different forms of fossil fuels.

Since the age of the dinosaurs, lots of carbon has been taken out of the atmosphere and turned into rocks, plants, and fossil fuels. As carbon left the atmosphere, the planet became less hot.

Brrr!

It's warm inside!

Hundreds of thousands of years ago

Hundreds of millions of years ago

Earth cooled down enough for ice to build up in the North and South Poles, creating ice ages! Dinosaurs were replaced with wooly mammoths, and eventually humans.

Cool, man!

Tens of thousands
of years ago

Two hundred
years ago

Since the last ice age the
planet has been fairly cool,
with lots of carbon buried
in the land and sea. But
about two hundred years
ago, people began digging
up fossil fuels from deep
underground for energy.

21

Inside fossil fuels are the solar energy captured by plants millions of years ago. People burn fossil fuels to release the energy. The energy can be used to power all sorts of things, like cars, factories, and power plants for electricity.

When fossil fuels are burned, the carbon inside them is released and goes back into the atmosphere. People are burning fossil fuels so quickly and putting so much carbon in the atmosphere that Earth is getting warmer fast.

Your elbow is in my butt again!

As Earth heats up, lots of things change.

Land and ocean temperatures go up.

Storms, droughts, and fires get stronger from all the heat energy.

24

Ice melts off land and flows into the oceans, making the seas rise.

The climate is changing.

The climate is now warming faster than Earth is able to cool down. It takes thousands to millions of years for Earth to change carbon dioxide into rocks and fossil fuels. Like a slow drain in an overflowing bathtub, the capture of carbon from the atmosphere is not fast enough to cool the planet down.

To cool the planet down, we need to stop putting so much carbon into the atmosphere. There are lots of ways to do this!

Most power plants today use fossil fuels like coal and methane gas to make electricity. Renewable energy like solar and wind power, which don't put carbon in the air, can be used instead.

This zero-carbon electricity can be used to power everything from trains and factories to heating and cooking in homes.

Building homes closer together with lots of walkways, bike paths, and electric buses means fewer cars using oil.

 Stopping deforestation and planting trees helps keep carbon in the plants and soil and out of the atmosphere.

 New ideas and inventions are happening every day to keep carbon in the ground!

How can you help cool the planet down?

You can go to a public meeting or start a petition asking organizations to use more clean energy.

With your friends you can write to or visit your local political representatives and tell them to act on climate.

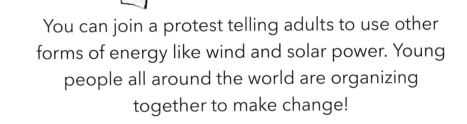

You can join a protest telling adults to use other forms of energy like wind and solar power. Young people all around the world are organizing together to make change!

Your elbow is still in my butt...

There is a lot you can do on your own, and even more you can do when you join other people.

THERE IS NO PLANET B

Like carbon you are powerful in numbers, and you can shape the whole world!

What's that smell?

SAVE OUR HOME

Fart!

Putting It All Together

Atoms are the building blocks of the world, so small you cannot see them. One of the most common atoms is **carbon**. You can find carbon in almost everything on the planet, including all living things. It really is the everywhere atom!

The amount of carbon on Earth does not change, meaning it is neither created nor destroyed. However, carbon changes form, such as from a gas to a plant. Carbon's journey is called the **carbon cycle**.

The carbon cycle affects how hot or cold Earth is over time, known as the **climate**. Earth's surface is surrounded by a thin layer of gases called the **atmosphere**. In the atmosphere, **greenhouse gases** trap heat from the sun, acting like a blanket to keep the planet warm. Two of the most common greenhouse gases have carbon atoms: carbon dioxide and methane. A lot of carbon in the atmosphere heats up the earth, like being under a thick blanket.

Early Earth had a lot of carbon in the atmosphere from all the volcanic activity. Volcanoes erupt magma and gases like carbon dioxide from the mantle below Earth's surface. All the carbon moving from inside the earth into the atmosphere made the planet very hot.

Over millions of years, a lot of carbon in the air turned into rock. This transformation happened through a process called **weathering**. During weathering, carbon mixes with rainwater, making it acidic, like soda water. As the rainwater falls, the acid breaks up and dissolves rocks and minerals into tiny pieces, like sugar mixing into water. The minerals and carbon wash down rivers into the ocean, where they are used by sea animals to make their shells. Over time the shells sink to the seafloor and are cemented together into layers of **limestone** rock. The weathering process is called the slow carbon cycle because it takes up to millions of years to happen.

Carbon is also taken out of the atmosphere by plants through **photosynthesis**. Plants use the sun's solar energy to transform water and carbon dioxide into plant food, called **glucose**. Plants use the glucose they make to grow and stay alive, releasing oxygen in the process.

Animals and humans cannot make their own food like plants do, so we eat plants or animals that eat plants. We eat to give our bodies energy to live and do things. In an almost mirror of photosynthesis, our bodies take in and transform oxygen and glucose into fuel. We exhale carbon dioxide back into the air, where plants can use it again for photosynthesis. Plants and animals that are not eaten break down, or **decay**, into the soil and atmosphere. Carbon moving from plants, animals, and the atmosphere is called the fast carbon cycle because it happens within years.

Plants also have a longer carbon cycle. Sometimes plants are buried without oxygen, which stops them from decaying back into the atmosphere. Instead, the plants and photosynthetic sea creatures called **plankton,** covered under layers of mud and rock and sand, are slowly cooked by heat and pressure, and over millions of years turn into **fossil fuels**.

Over two million years ago, so much carbon had transformed from a gas into rocks and fossil fuels that the world cooled down. As Earth cooled, the temperature of the planet was mainly ruled by small changes in its position as it circled the sun. These changes affected how much of the sun's heat reached the tips of the planet, the **poles**. Less sunlight led to the growth of large ice sheets at the poles, called an **ice age**. More sunlight shrank the ice sheets, creating what's called an **interglacial period**. This was the cycle for millions of years.

Today Earth's climate is no longer ruled by natural forces, but by human activity, through the burning of fossil fuels. Fossil fuels contain the tightly packed, solar-powered energy of prehistoric life. By the 1800s people were digging up more and more fossil fuels to build and power the modern world, including electricity, cars, and factories.

Since fossil fuels are ancient life, they contain carbon. When fossil fuels are burned, that carbon is released into the atmosphere. All the carbon in the atmosphere is warming up the planet. The extra heat has many negative effects, such as more heat waves and droughts, stronger forest fires, more powerful and destructive storms, and sea-level rise from ice melting off of land. Scientists warn that if the planet gets too hot, it could lead to even more serious and damaging effects.

To prevent Earth from getting too hot, we need to stop putting so much carbon into the atmosphere. Fossil fuels are the main source of this carbon. We burn fossil fuels to use the energy, but there are other forms of energy. Solar and wind energy, for example, are **carbon-free** energy because they do not put carbon into the atmosphere. Using carbon-free energy can help cool the planet. People all over the world are working to replace fossil-fuel energy with carbon-free energy. ◆

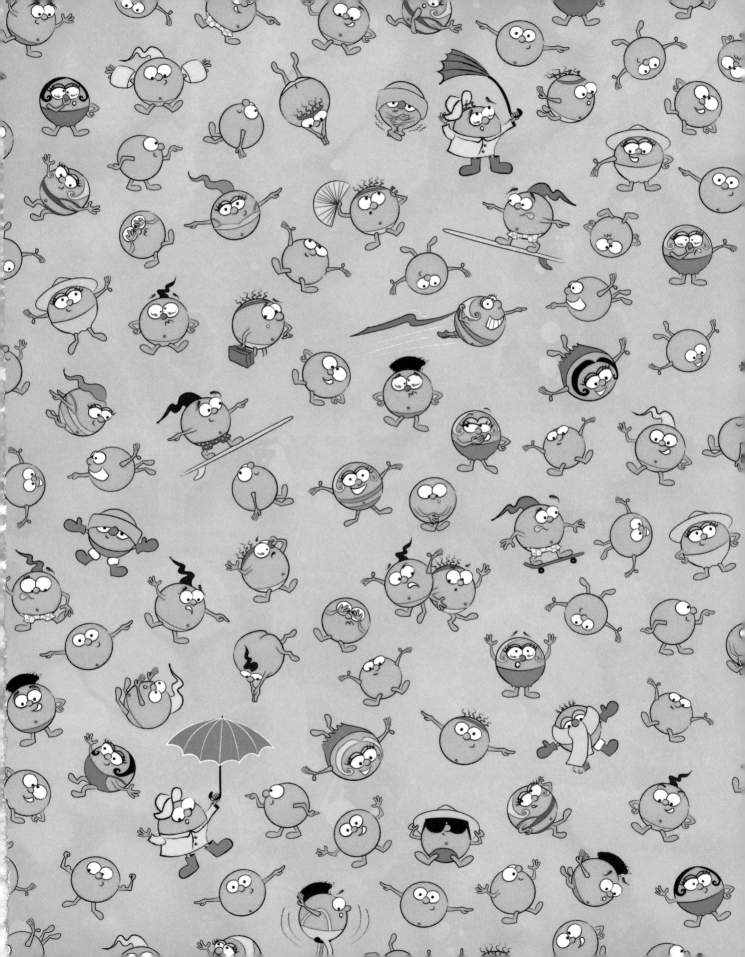

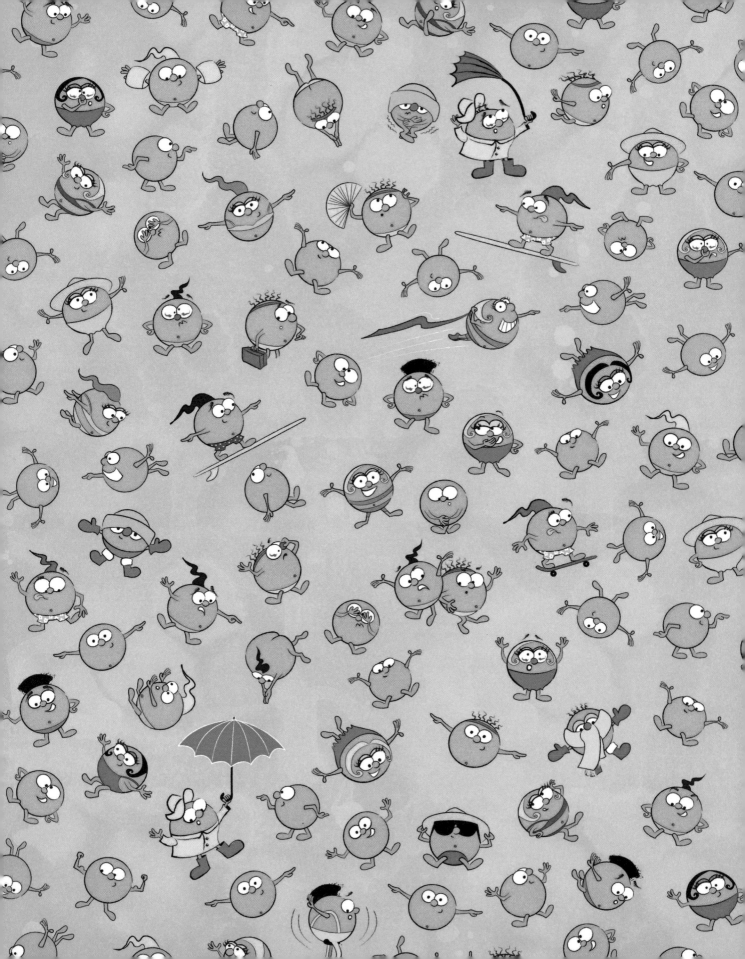